MW01292131

This book belongs to:

____

Made in United States
Orlando, FL
21 November 2022

24824674R00065